Light and Dark

IT'S SCIENCE!

Light and Dark

Sally Hewitt

CHILDREN'S PRESS®

A Division of Grolier Publishing

NEW YORK • LONDON • HONG KONG • SYDNEY
DANBURY, CONNECTICUT

This edition published in 2007 by Franklin Watts
338 Euston Rd
London NW1 3BH

Franklin Watts Australia
Level 17/207 Kent St
Sydney NSW 2000

Series editor: Rachel Cooke
Designer: Mo Choy
Picture research: Susan Mennell
Photography: Ray Moller unless otherwise acknowledged
Consultant: Sally Nankivell-Aston
Copyright © Franklin Watts 1998

A CIP catalogue record for this book
is available from the British Library.

ISBN 978 0 7496 7773 2

Dewey Classification 535

Printed in Malaysia

Acknowledgements:
Bruce Coleman pp. 9br (Alain Compost), 11bl (Kevin Rushby), 11br (Charles and Sandra Hood),
12t (Felix Labhardt), 27tl (Kim Taylor), 27tr (M. Fogden), 27bl (M. Fogden);
Robert Harding pp. 17t (Mark Stephenson) 24t (J.M. Francillon);
Image Bank pp. 7 (Alain Choisnet), 10t (Max Dannenbaum), 10b (F. D'Elbee), 20tl (Joseph van Os);
Oxford Scientific Films p. 20tr (Harold Taylor); Tony Stone Images p.17br (Terry Vine).
Thank you to Tridias, 6 Bennett Street, Bath BA1 2QP, 01225 314730 for their help with the objects
photographed for this book on pp. 14, 19 and 26.
Thanks as well to our models: Miles Wong-Tester, James Moller,
Nakita Ogugua, Luke Richardson and Charlotte Harrison.
Franklin Watts is a division of Hachette Children's Books, an Hachette Livre UK company.

Contents

Light and Dark

In the **daytime**, the **sun** lights up the **earth** and we can see what is happening all around us.

At night when the sun goes down, the earth becomes dark. We have to find ways of lighting up the dark so that we can see.

 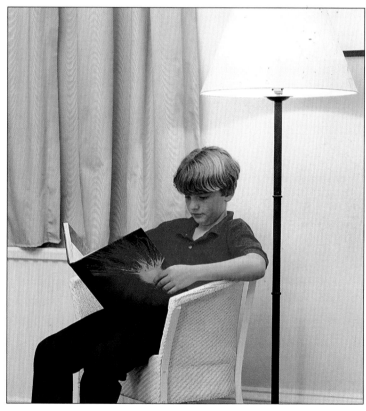

THINK ABOUT IT!

Do you play games or read during dark evenings?

What could you do in the evening if you couldn't light up the dark?

Street lights and car headlights help to light up the dark.

What other ways can you think of to do this?

 TRY IT OUT!

At **nighttime**, close the curtains and turn out the light in your bedroom. Is there any light getting in? What can you see?

Turn on the light. What can you see now?

Daylight

The sun is a gigantic
ball of hot, burning gas.
The earth is a ball of rock,
much smaller than the sun.
The sun is a long way from
our planet Earth, but it gives
us heat and light.

Each day the earth turns around.
During the day, the part of Earth
we live on faces the sun.
At night, it faces away.

 TRY IT OUT!

Pretend a ball is the earth.
Make a drawing of yourself, cut it out,
and stick it on the ball. Hold the ball up
in the sun, so that one side is brightly lit.
Turn the ball around gradually—watch
yourself move from daytime into night.

The sun is up and it is daytime.
What are the people who use these
things doing today?
What do you do during the day?

💡 THINK ABOUT IT!

Why do you think that most people and animals are
awake during the day and asleep at night? Can
you think of any animals that are awake at night?

9

Darkness

At night we can see the **moon** shining in the sky.

The moon is a dark, cold ball of rock, like the earth.
The sun shines on it and makes it look bright.

 THINK ABOUT IT!

On a cloudy night, we cannot see any light from the moon.
It is very dark.
What happens to sunlight on a cloudy day?

When you shut your eyes, your eyelids keep the light out of your eyes. Shut your eyes. Can you see anything?

Why do you think it so dark in a cave and at the bottom of the sea?

 TRY IT OUT!

Try making a very dark corner, like this one, in your bedroom by keeping out as much light as you can.

 LOOK AGAIN

Look again at page 7. How do we light up the dark?

Casting Shadows

Can you see how light **rays** come from the sun in straight lines?

Rays of light cannot bend, go around corners, or shine through a solid object like you!

 TRY IT OUT!

On a sunny day, stand with your back to the sun. Because the sun cannot shine through you, your body will cast a dark **shadow**. Move around and watch your shadow do the same things as you.

Light from a candle shines out all around it. Look at the shadows of the mugs falling in every direction.

A beam from a flashlight only shines where you point it. What has happened to the shadows of the mugs now?

TRY IT OUT!

Make a shadow puppet show. Cut out cardboard figures like these and tape them on to a stick. Shine a bright light onto a wall and hold the figures in front of the light. Move them around and start your show!

Seeing

We see when light shines on to the things around us and into our open eyes.
We can see shapes and colors, and we can tell how far away things are.

Paul is walking to the table. What can
he see around him?

💡 **THINK ABOUT IT!**

How would Paul get safely to the table if he had his eyes shut?
Why would it be much harder?

The colored circle in your eye is the **iris**. The black circle, called the **pupil**, is a hole in the iris. You see when light shines through your pupils into your eye.

The iris can make the pupil bigger to let in more light. It can also make the pupil smaller to keep light out.

pupil

iris

 TRY IT OUT!

Look out of the window on a sunny day or into a brightly lit room. Now look at your pupils in a mirror. Note what size they are.

Look into a dark place for a few moments. Look at your pupils: are they bigger or smaller? They will probably have opened up to let in as much light as possible.

15

Reflection

When you look into a mirror, you can see your **reflection**.

TRY IT OUT!

Collect some objects like the ones on this page. Look at them and feel them.

Do they look dull or shiny?
Do they feel rough or smooth?
Can you see your reflection when you look at them?
Which one is the smoothest, shiniest object?
Which one shows you the clearest reflection of your face?

THINK ABOUT IT!

Write your name and look at its reflection in a mirror. What is different about the reflection? Does the same thing happen with your reflection?

You can see clear reflections in still water.

Wind ripples the water and spoils the reflections.

 TRY IT OUT!

Find a puddle after it has rained and the sun is shining. Can you see a clear reflection of yourself in the puddle? Ripple the puddle with your hand. What happens to your reflection now?

Shining Through

Different things happen to light when it shines onto a book, a window, and a mesh curtain because they are all made of different materials.

A book is **opaque**. You cannot see through it and light cannot shine through it.

Glass is **transparent**. You can see through it and light shines through it.

This mesh curtain is **translucent**. It lets some light shine though.

👁 LOOK AGAIN

Look again at page 12 to find something opaque, and at page 10 to find something translucent.

All these things are made of different materials.

TRY IT OUT!

Make a collection of things like the ones in the picture.

Hold each one up to the light. Which ones can you see through?

Shine a flashlight onto them. Which ones does the light shine through?
Which ones cast a shadow?

Separate them into groups of opaque objects, transparent objects,
and translucent objects.

Bigger and Smaller

A **lens** is a curved piece of transparent material such as glass or plastic. Lenses can make things look bigger or smaller, nearer or farther away.

There are lenses in **binoculars**, a **microscope,** and a **magnifying glass**.

If you look through the narrow end of a pair of binoculars, things look nearer. If you look through the wide end, things look farther away.

A microscope makes tiny things look big enough to see clearly.

A magnifying glass makes small things look bigger.

 TRY IT OUT!

Make a collection of small things and
look at them through a magnifying glass.
Look at your skin, nails, and hair as well.

Special lenses inside our eyes let us see things sharply. The lenses in
some people's eyes do not work properly so they have to wear
glasses or contact lenses.

Glasses have lenses inside
them that help people to see
more clearly.
Contact lenses work in
the same way but
they are put straight
onto the eye.

Snapshots

Photographs
are easy
to take.
First, load
the film into
a camera.

Next, look through the eyepiece to find the
picture you want and press the shutter button.
A shutter will blink open to let light in through
the camera lens onto the film.
This records the image.

Have the film
developed to
get a print of the
photograph you took.

 LOOK AGAIN

Look again at page 15 to
find out how light reaches
the lenses in your eyes.

22

A moving image is made by taking a series of still pictures like these very quickly with a special movie camera.

The pictures are projected onto a screen one after the other so quickly that you see the girl running along.

 TRY IT OUT!

Fold a piece of thin white paper in half.
Copy the sleepy face onto the bottom half of the paper.
Trace the face onto the top half but add open eyes.
Pull the bottom corner up and down very fast—watch the eyes open and shut!

23

Rainbows

We call light from the sun white light because it looks white.

When it is raining and sunlight shines through raindrops, the white light is split into the seven different colors of the **rainbow**: red, orange, yellow, green, blue, indigo, and violet.

 TRY IT OUT!

Blow some bubbles in the sunlight.
Can you see rainbows in the bubbles?

The colors of the rainbow can be mixed together to make white!

 TRY IT OUT!

You will need:
– white oaktag
– tracing paper
– felt-tip pens the colors of the rainbow
– a pencil
– scissors

Trace this circle onto the white oaktag.

Color in the segments.
Make the colors as bright as you can.

Cut out the circle and carefully push the pencil through the center.

Spin the circle and watch the colors of the rainbow turn white.

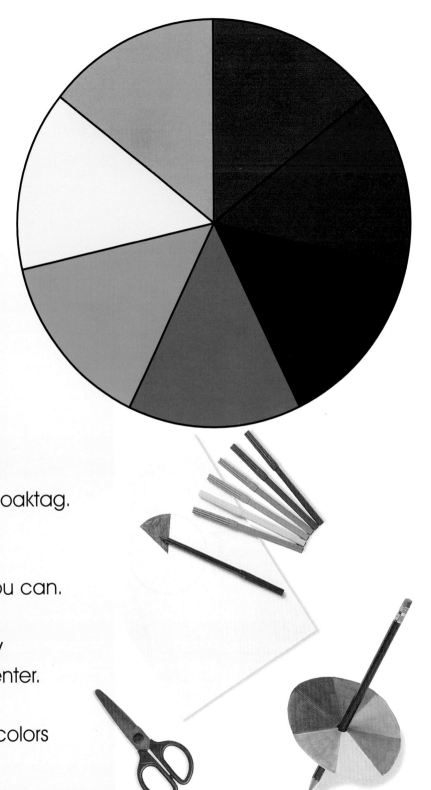

A Colorful World

The world is a colorful place. Can you see
all the colors of the rainbow in this picture?
What other colors can you see?

 THINK ABOUT IT!

Imagine what the world would be
like if there were no colors and
everything was black and white!

Animals, plants, and insects use color in all kinds of different ways.

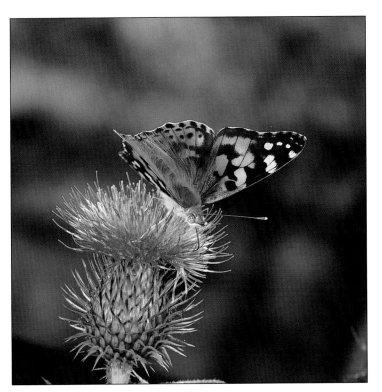

Insects are attracted by colorful flowers. The bright colors tell them that they will find something good to eat.

It is difficult to see a green snake hiding among the leaves.

The bright yellow and black stripes of this frog warn hungry animals that it is poisonous to eat.

 LOOK AGAIN

Look again through this book. What blue, red, and yellow things can you find?

Useful words

Binoculars Binoculars help you to see things that are too far away to see clearly with your eyes alone. Binoculars make things look nearer.

Daytime Daytime begins when the sun rises in the morning and ends when the sun sets in the evening. It is light during daytime.

Earth Earth is where we live. It is a large ball of rock called a planet. The earth gets its heat and light from the sun, which it slowly moves around. The earth turns around once each day.

Iris The iris is the colored part of your eye. It has a black hole in its center called the **pupil**. The iris controls the size of the pupil.

Lens A lens is a curved piece of see-through or transparent material. Depending on its shape, a lens makes things look bigger or smaller.

Magnifying glass A magnifying glass is something you look through to make small things look bigger.

Microscope A microscope makes things that are too small to see clearly with just your eyes look much, much bigger.

Moon The moon is a ball or rock that moves around the earth. Nothing lives on the moon. We can only see it when it is lit up by the sun.

Nighttime Nighttime begins when the sun sets in the evening and ends when the sun rises in the morning. It is dark during nighttime.

Opaque Opaque is something that light cannot shine through.

Photograph A photograph is a print of a picture taken by a camera. Light goes through the camera lens onto a film, which is changed by the light.

Pupil The pupil is the part of the eye that looks black. It is really a hole that light can shine through.

Rainbow A rainbow is the bow-shaped arc formed when sunlight shines through raindrops and splits into seven different colors.

Ray A ray is a straight line of light that comes from a bright object.

Reflection A reflection appears when light rays bounce, or reflect, off a shiny surface like a mirror. The picture you see has its parts reversed.

Shadow A shadow is a patch of darkness made when light cannot shine through a solid object.

Sun The sun is the huge ball of burning gases that gives heat and light to the earth.

Translucent Translucent is something that only some light can shine through.

Transparent Transparent is something that all light can shine through.

Index

About this book

Children are natural scientists. They learn by touching and feeling, noticing, asking questions, and trying things out for themselves. The books in the *It's Science!* series are designed for the way children learn. Familiar objects are used as starting points for further learning. *Light and dark* starts with daylight and explores the concepts of light and color.

Each double page spread introduces a new topic, such as reflection. Information is given, questions are asked, and activities are suggested that encourage children to make discoveries and develop new ideas for themselves.
Look out for these panels throughout the book:

TRY IT OUT! indicates a simple activity, using safe materials, that proves or explores a point.
THINK ABOUT IT! indicates a question inspired by the information on the page but that points the reader to areas not covered by the book.
LOOK AGAIN introduces a cross-referencing activity that links themes and facts through the book.

Encourage children not to take the familiar world for granted. Point things out, ask questions, and enjoy making scientific discoveries together.